latin

latin

a culinary journey of discovery

ELISABETH LUARD

Love Food® is an imprint of Parragon Books Ltd

Parragon
Queen Street House
4 Queen Street
Bath BA1 1HE, UK

Copyright © Parragon Books Ltd 2007

Love Food® and the accompanying heart device is a trademark of Parragon Books Ltd

ISBN: 978-1-4054-9562-2
Printed in China

Produced by the Bridgewater Book Company Ltd

Photography: Laurie Evans
Home economist: Carol Tennant

Notes for the Reader
This book uses imperial, metric, and US cup measurements. Follow the same units of measurement throughout; do not mix imperial and metric. All spoon measurements are level: teaspoons are assumed to be 5 ml, and tablespoons are assumed to be 15 ml. Unless otherwise stated, milk is assumed to be whole, eggs and individual vegetables such as potatoes are medium, and pepper is freshly ground black pepper. Recipes using raw or very lightly cooked eggs and those using raw or very lightly cooked fish should be avoided by infants, the elderly, pregnant women, convalescents, and anyone suffering from an illness. The times given are an approximate guide only.

Picture Acknowledgments
The publisher would like to thank Envision/Corbis for permission to reproduce copyright material on page 32.

Contents

Introduction

The cooking of Latin America is both comfortingly familiar and excitingly exotic. Take a basketful of ingredients found nowhere else on the earth and add the knowledge of a variety of indigenous local food experts and the result, unsurprisingly, is a mix-and-match cuisine that is varied, complex, and capable of a high degree of sophistication.

The pre-Columbian diet

The early civilizations of the region—Olmec, Maya, and Aztec in Central America and the Inca in Peru—knew how to make their raw materials palatable. This was just as well, since, in their untreated form, some were not well adapted to the human digestive tract (corn and cassava or *manioc*), others were not fit for purpose unless subjected to serious preparation methods (vanilla and chocolate), and some were downright poisonous (the toxic, bitter cassava).

After the arrival of the Europeans some five centuries ago, during the course of what became known as the Columbian Exchange, recipes and ingredients were traded back and forth between the Old World and the New until the threads became so inextricably tangled that it is impossible to tell where one tradition ends and the other begins. Who is to say if the seviches of Mexico and Guatemala are more closely related to the vinegar pickles of Spain than they are to the marinated raw fish enjoyed by the Maya? And who would have thought that the native annatto, a seed favored for coloring and flavoring

by the Aztecs, would be used as a handy substitute for Spanish saffron, as well as to reproduce the sunny color of dende oil—an ingredient of purely African origin? Coffee, bananas, and coconut, now common crops throughout the region, were unknown in pre-Columbian times.

The Columbian Exchange

The two-way transatlantic traffic continued throughout the colonial period—roughly 1500 to 1900—bringing New World ingredients to Old World pantries. It is hard to imagine the diet of Europe and Asia—or even that of the North Americans—without potatoes, corn, cannellini beans, tomatoes, chocolate, avocados, pumpkins, and squash, not to mention the mighty and mightily addictive chile. In return, the Old World supplied cattle for milk and meat, sheep for wool, and cheese, pigs, poultry, and the main Eurasian staple grains, wheat and rice. Most important of all to a people who never invented the wheel, the Europeans introduced a means of transport, the horse, providing a method of moving men and goods across land rather than water.

Materials and the means to move them were not the only consequence of the Exchange. Since the early colonizers were either soldiers without their wives or unmarried priests, local cooks were pressed into service, which led to the interweaving of culinary culture that persists to this day.

Influential ingredients

Geography and latitude dictate the raw materials of the Latin American kitchen. The continent, north to south, runs across both hemispheres, and the lands of the Latins, the regions colonized by Spain and Portugal, stretch from the steamy tropics to the polar ice cap—to the east, the rainforests of the Amazon; to the west, the deserts of the high Andes. The common link, the coastline, fronts two oceans, the Atlantic and the Pacific. Geographical diversity, along with the relatively late appearance of human settlement and the difficulty of communication between one group and another unless by water, led to the development of a wide variety of habitats unaltered by the presence of man.

Nevertheless, long before the arrival of Europeans in Latin America, the indigenous inhabitants were already cultivating sophisticated strains of edible plant foods unknown anywhere else on the earth, developing ways of processing foodstuffs which, in their untreated state, were at best unpalatable and at worst deadly. The most useful and easy to grow, such as corn, beans, and potatoes, quickly became staples to fill the world's pantry; others, including tomatoes, avocados and squashes, became popular because they tasted good. The chile, a pepper substitute much welcomed by the poor of Asia and Europe, since true pepper was not only hard to obtain but prohibitively expensive, was modified to produce the mild salad and cooking peppers, a form in which they were re-exported to their land of origin.

Even today, many of the vegetables and grains of the region remain more or less unexploited outside their home territory, sometimes because they occupy a specific botanical niche that cannot be reproduced elsewhere, but more often because their preparation and usefulness is little understood.

Regional differences and similarities

Within all this diversity, the culinary habits of the 26 sovereign nations that make up the modern population of Latin America are, if not identical, remarkably compatible.

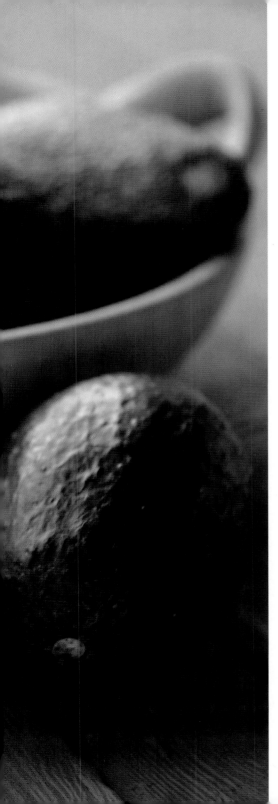

The unifying element—habitats being so diverse and the native population being widely dispersed—was the Columbian Exchange that began in 1492.

The traditional diet of the indigenous peoples was based on the trinity of corn, beans, and potatoes, with cassava grown wherever none of these three could survive. This simple but nourishing diet was balanced by a wide variety of gourds and greens that could be cultivated in association with the main staple foodstuffs, supplemented by wild gatherings—game, insects, reptiles, fish and shellfish, seaweeds, herbs, and fungi. Meat, barbecued or cooked in an earth oven (usually as part of religious celebrations), was consumed only at festivals and on days when offerings were made to the gods.

In the post-Columbian kitchen, the strength of the culinary habit lies in an understanding of what combines well with what. Foods that taste good together are presented together, although not necessarily cooked together. You will find no complicated sauces or flavoring reductions, and, with the exception of desserts, very little that demands enrichment with butter or cream. Cheese, both fresh and sharp, is usually presented as a side dish, as an enhancement to the main dish, or as a meat substitute. Meat is prepared according to the ancient tradition of game cooking; creatures of uncertain age and provenance are cooked long and gently in a closed pot. Fish, on the other hand, is cooked as briefly as possible and sometimes not at all. Lake and river fish are rarely eaten fresh but dried for preservation without salt, though the flavor is strong and you are unlikely to find the product outside Latin America.

Legumes and starch foods are often eaten together, either in the form of wraps, as with Mexico's tortillas with black beans, or in meatless stews, such as the beans and corn dishes of Chile, Ecuador, and Bolivia. Amazonia has dishes made with cassava, the starch vegetable of the tropics. Potatoes are the mainstay of the Andean uplands, with the vast pine forests of southern Chile providing pine nuts as the traditional source of protein. The gauchos of Argentina, southern Brazil, and Uruguay prefer a diet of meat from their wandering herds of European cattle, reluctantly adding vegetables if there is no other option. Elsewhere, vegetables are presented without apology as dishes in their own right—there is no need for meat or fish when there are bean and grain recipes to satisfy the most demanding diner.

Chile, ground or crumbled and used in much the same way as freshly milled pepper, is the traditional seasoning for both sweet and savory foods (salt and sugar was added to the diet in colonial times). Desserts are mostly Hispanic in origin, a repertoire of custards and pastries, secrets of which were passed from the Moors of Andalusia to the convent cooks of Christian Spain and Portugal. Intoxicants native to the region include a beer made with the fermented sap of the maguey cactus; a chewing leaf, coca; and *mate* (pronounced ma-tay), a mildly stimulating infusion from the leaves of a desert shrub.

Fruit is the most widely available street food in tropical territory; you will find it at corner kiosks and in breakfast bars throughout Central America, cut into chunks or freshly squeezed to order. In the markets of the big cities, street food is anything that is portable enough to be held in the hand and makes the most of whatever is cheap and in season, such as tamales—corn flour dumplings stuffed with a little chile-spiked stew, or tacos—soft tortilla wraps filled with shredded chicken or pork. In Rio, carnival food is a fritter pan-fried in dende oil and made with ground black-eyed peas and little scarlet shrimp caught on the shoreline, to be dried in heaps in the sun. Along the coast of Chile, where much of the population lives within a mile or two of the ocean, street food is freshly opened shellfish—oysters, abalone, and razorshells.

Latin American cooking today

The traditional Latin American kitchen is a marriage of knowledge and skill, with little in the way of artistry; ingredients are chosen with care and prepared with simplicity, then left to speak for themselves. This is not necessarily obvious when you consider chili con carne, beans and rice, and tortilla wraps—recipes that have long been popular as street corner fast food and backyard cookouts.

The domestic cooking of Latin America is less well known. While the culinary habits of Mexico, Brazil, and the Caribbean are those most frequently encountered outside the territory, there are many good things to be found in the kitchens of Colombia, Venezuela, Peru, Ecuador, Chile, Argentina, Paraguay, and Uruguay.

Every region has its own distinctive ingredients and recipes. Many of the differences are the result of variations in climate and exterior influences from the colonists. The indigenous civilizations exchanged culinary knowledge over thousands of years: the Mayans imported the Peruvian upward-pointing, torpedo-shaped chile from the Incas and crossed it with Mexico's downward-dropping, lantern shaped chile; both are fiery and together they are the ancestors of all our modern mild (as well as hot) capsicums.

While the region's traditional dishes are prepared to recipes handed down from one generation to another, the culinary culture continues to evolve—populations migrate and new kids arrive on the block. Nuevo Latino, or modernized traditional, is a style growing in popularity south of the Rio Grande as well as in the sophisticated restaurants of Los Angeles, Miami, and New York. Rules are made to be broken. So if you can't find exactly the right ingredient or you simply want to present your dish in a new way, join the club—adapt, invent, and enjoy!

Appetizers and Snacks

Throughout the region, the menu of the day is not so much a series of main events as several moments that bridge the gap between the dawn to midday period, when heavy bean and grain dishes are traditionally served, and dusk, when something light is eaten.

Among those dishes that are regarded as snacks to be eaten during the day as well as being suitable to serve as a first course are the classic *seviche*, marinated raw fish, and *escabeche*, cooked fresh fish pickled in a spiced vinegar. Then there are foods that can be held in the hand, such as the ever-popular *quesadillas* and *empanadas*, offering delicious filling encased in pastry parcels. Also included are simple stock-based soups.

Lime-marinated swordfish with shrimp

Seviche de pez-espada con camarones

Serves 4 to 6

12 oz/350 g swordfish steaks

9 oz/250 g raw shrimp

juice of 3 limes

1 tsp sea salt

2 tbsp coarsely chopped fresh cilantro leaves

1 green or red chile, seeded and finely chopped

2 tbsp diced papaya or avocado (optional)

For serving

lime quarters

unsalted tortilla chips or soft cornmeal tortillas

The fish and shellfish effectively "cook" in the citrus juice in which they are marinated, without the application of heat— a method also used by the fishermen of the South Seas, early colonizers of America's Pacific coastline.

Remove the skin and bones from the fish steaks. Cut the fish into neat, bite-size pieces, removing any stray bones, and transfer to a nonreactive bowl.

Remove the heads and tails of the shrimp, then peel. If large, remove the black intestinal vein that runs down the back by pulling on the center of the tail fin. Save the shells for making a stock.

Add the shrimp to the fish with two-thirds of the lime juice and the salt and gently combine. Cover the bowl with plastic wrap and let marinate in the salad compartment of the refrigerator for 2 to 3 hours, or until the fish and shellfish are opaque.

Drain, discarding the juices, and dress with the remaining lime juice, cilantro, and chile. Fold in the papaya, if using.

Serve at room temperature with lime quarters and unsalted tortilla chips, or soft tortillas cut into bite-size triangles or squares and sautéed in a little vegetable oil until crisp.

Spice-pickled bonito or tuna

Escabeche de bonito o atún

A herby pickling vinegar adds flavor and a little shelf life to the fisherman's catch. The technique was developed in the days when refrigeration wasn't an option, but the result tasted so good that the recipe has stayed on the menu.

Serves 4 to 6

1 lb 2 oz/500 g bonito or tuna steaks (or any firm-fleshed fish)

2 tbsp all-purpose flour

2 to 3 tbsp olive oil

salt and pepper

Marinade

1 onion, finely sliced

1 garlic clove, crushed

1 small carrot, scraped and diced

1 tbsp dried oregano, crumbled

1 tsp coriander seeds, coarsely crushed

1 fresh or dried red chile, seeded and chopped

4 tbsp wine vinegar or lemon juice

For serving

1 lb 2 oz/500 g fresh or canned red bell peppers

1 to 2 tbsp olive oil

crisp lettuce leaves

soft cornmeal tortillas or arepas (Chilean tortillas)

Remove the skin and bones from the fish steaks. Cut the fish into neat strips, removing any stray bones, and transfer to a nonreactive bowl. Sprinkle lightly with salt, cover, and let stand at room temperature for 10 minutes to firm up. Drain off any liquid.

Spread the flour on a plate and season with salt and pepper to taste. Flip the fish strips through the seasoned flour.

Heat the oil in a large skillet until hot, add a few strips of the fish and cook over medium-high heat, turning once, for 1 to 2 minutes—just long enough to brown the coating and firm the flesh. Carefully transfer the strips to a shallow dish, arranging them in a single layer. Repeat until all the fish strips are cooked.

Reheat the skillet with its oily juices, add the onion, garlic, and carrot and cook over medium heat, stirring, for a few moments to blend the flavors. Add the oregano, coriander, chile, vinegar, and a splash of water. Let bubble fiercely for a few minutes to soften the vegetables, then pour the contents of the skillet over the fish and turn gently in the vinegar mixture. Cover the dish with plastic wrap and let marinate in a cool place for at least 4 hours, or preferably overnight.

Meanwhile, prepare the red bell peppers, if serving. If fresh, preheat the oven to 450°F/230°C, put on a baking sheet, and roast for 10 to 15 minutes, or until the flesh is tender and the skins are black and blistered in places. Transfer to a plastic bag and let stand for 10 minutes to loosen the skins. Remove the skins and seeds. Cut the flesh into strips and dress with the oil. If canned, drain, cut into strips and dress with the oil.

Scatter the red pepper strips over the fish and serve with crisp lettuce leaves and soft tortillas or arepas for scooping.

Cheese turnovers with chili sauce

Quesadillas

Makes 12

vegetable oil, for pan-frying
or oiling

milk, for brushing (optional)

Pie dough

2½ cups white bread flour,
plus extra for dusting

½ tsp salt

4 tbsp olive oil

about ⅔ cup hot water

Filling

4 tbsp grated queso Oaxaca or
Gruyère cheese

5½ oz/150 g requesón or
ricotta cheese

1 tsp finely chopped green chile

1 tbsp chopped fresh cilantro

Chili sauce

1 lb 2 oz/500 g fresh ripe tomatoes,
peeled and diced, or canned
chopped tomatoes

1 fresh or dried red chile, seeded
and chopped

1 garlic clove, chopped

1 tbsp olive oil

Here, creamy little mouthfuls of cheese are enclosed in a crisp pastry coating. The pie dough, made with hot water and olive oil, is robust enough to withstand pan-frying, but it can be baked instead.

First make the pie dough. Sift the flour and salt into a bowl. Using your hands, work in the olive oil and enough hot water to make a fairly soft, smooth dough that comes away from the side of the bowl. Alternatively, use a food processor to make the dough. Form the dough into a ball, wrap in plastic wrap, and let rest in a cool place for 30 minutes.

Meanwhile, make the filling and prepare the sauce. Mash the cheeses together with the chile and cilantro in a separate bowl and set aside. Put all the sauce ingredients in a blender or food processor and blend to a purée. Transfer to a small saucepan and let bubble for 10 minutes, or until you have a thick dipping sauce. Set aside to cool.

Turn the dough out on to a floured board, roll it into a sausage shape, and cut into 12 equal-size pieces. With the tips of your fingers, knead each piece into a small ball. Roll or pat each ball into a thin round the size of a large saucer—you will find it easier to roll if you sandwich it between 2 sheets of plastic wrap.

Drop a teaspoon of the filling off-center on to each round, leaving a wide margin all around. Make a dip in the center of the filling and add a dab of the sauce. Dampen the edge of each round, fold in half to enclose the filling, and press the edges together to seal.

When all the quesadillas are prepared, heat a finger's depth of oil in a large skillet over medium-high heat. When hot, add the quesadillas, in small batches, to the oil and cook for 2 minutes on each side, or until crisp and brown. Remove and drain on paper towels.

Alternatively, to bake the quesadillas, preheat the oven to 375°F/190°C. Arrange in neat lines on an oiled baking sheet, brush the tops with a little milk, and prick with a fork. Bake in the preheated oven for 15 to 20 minutes, or until well puffed and golden.

Serve the quesadillas hot, while the filling is still creamy and runny, with the extra sauce as a dip.

Crab and chile pasties

Empanadas de cangrejo

Serves 4 to 6

vegetable oil, for oiling

milk, for brushing

Filling

9 oz/250 g prepared fresh crabmeat

2 tbsp olive oil

2 garlic cloves, chopped

2 green chiles, seeded
and chopped

1 green bell pepper, seeded
and diced

2 tbsp diced tomato or
1 tbsp tomato paste

1 tbsp pitted olives, chopped

Pie dough

2 cups white bread flour, plus extra
for dusting

1 tsp baking powder

1/2 tsp salt

7 tbsp lard, chilled and diced

1 large egg

1 egg yolk

For serving (optional)

1 ripe avocado, pitted, peeled,
and mashed

juice of 1 lime

1 tbsp chopped fresh cilantro

These crisp, lard-shortened pastry parcels contain fresh-picked crabmeat—spider crabs are perfect—flavored with garlic, chile, and olives. You can use ready-made pie dough if you prefer.

First make the filling. Pick over the crabmeat and remove any stray pieces of shell. Heat the oil in a skillet, add the garlic, chiles, and green bell pepper and cook over medium heat, stirring frequently, for 4 to 5 minutes, or until the vegetables are softened. Add the tomato and heat until bubbling, mashing to blend. Stir in the crabmeat and olives and bubble up again. Set aside to cool while you make the dough.

Sift the flour, baking powder, and salt into a large bowl. With a sharp knife, chop the lard into the flour until it resembles rough oatmeal. Beat the egg and egg yolk together with a fork, then work lightly into the flour mixture with the knife or your fingertips, adding enough cold water to make a fairly soft, smooth dough. Alternatively, use a food processor to make the dough. Form the dough into a ball and brush the outside with oil or wrap in plastic wrap. Let rest in a cool place for 30 minutes.

Preheat the oven to 375°F/190°C. Roll the dough out on a floured board to a thickness of about 1/4 inch/5 mm. Use a wine glass to cut out small rounds—choose the size you want. Put a dab of the crab mixture on each round. Dampen the edge of each round, fold in half to enclose the filling, and press the edges together to seal. Arrange in neat lines on an oiled baking sheet, brush the tops with milk, and prick with a fork.

Bake in the preheated oven for 15 to 20 minutes, or until crisp and golden. If you like, serve with a dipping salsa of the avocado mixed with the lime juice and cilantro.

Potato cakes with peanut salsa

Llapingachos con ají de maní

Serves 4 to 6

4 large starchy potatoes, scrubbed and quartered

2 tbsp grated cheddar-type cheese

2 tbsp finely chopped fresh cilantro

1 red or green chile, seeded and finely chopped

1 large egg, beaten

vegetable oil, for cooking

salt

Peanut salsa

1¹/2 cups roasted peanuts or coarse peanut butter

2 tbsp lemon juice

1 tsp unrefined cane sugar

4 yellow or red chiles, seeded

1 red bell pepper, seeded and chopped

2 tbsp ricotta cheese

¹/2 tsp salt

Ecuadorian fast food, these little potato cakes have a satisfyingly rough texture that works perfectly with the grainy, nut-thickened dipping sauce called *ají de mani*.

Cook the potatoes in their skins in a large saucepan of salted boiling water for 20 minutes, or until tender. Drain, reserving about ²/3 cup of the cooking water. As soon as the potatoes are cool enough to handle, remove the skins. Set aside two of the potato quarters, then mash the remainder coarsely with a fork in a bowl. Using your hands but without crushing out all the lumps, work in the cheese, cilantro, chile, egg, and a little salt.

Put all the salsa ingredients in a blender or food processor with the reserved potato and potato cooking water and blend to a purée. Transfer to a saucepan and heat gently until bubbling.

When ready to cook, heat a finger's depth of oil in a large skillet over medium-high heat. When hot, gently drop tablespoonfuls of the potato cake mixture, in small batches, into the oil, flatten with the back of the spoon, and cook until the undersides are golden and crisp. Turn carefully and cook on the other side. Remove and drain on paper towels.

Serve the potato cakes hot, with the salsa separately for dipping, or drop a teaspoon of the sauce on top of each potato cake.

Potato cornmeal bread with pine nuts

Chapale chileno

Serves 4 to 6

butter or lard, for greasing

2 lb 4 oz/1 kg starchy potatoes, scrubbed

3/4 oz ground cornmeal

4 tbsp grated cheddar-type cheese

2 tbsp toasted pine nuts

1 tsp dried chile flakes

1 large egg, beaten

salt

chili sauce, for serving

This Chilean spoon bread, thickened with potato and enriched with cheese and pine nuts, is baked in a roasting pan and eaten with a shake of chili sauce.

Preheat the oven to 350°F/180°C. Grease a rectangular roasting pan with butter or lard.

Cook the potatoes in their skins in a large saucepan of salted boiling water for 20 minutes, or until tender. Drain, reserving the cooking water. As soon as the potatoes are cool enough to handle, remove the skins. Mash the potatoes coarsely with a fork in a bowl. Using your hands but without crushing out all the lumps, work in the cornmeal, cheese, most of the pine nuts, chile flakes, egg, a little salt, and enough of the reserved potato cooking water to make a fairly soft dough.

Spread the dough out in the prepared pan and level off the top. Sprinkle with the remaining pine nuts, pressing them lightly into the surface. Bake in the preheated oven for 45 to 50 minutes, or until the top is brown and crisp and the dough is firm. Cut into squares and eat with a shake of chili sauce.

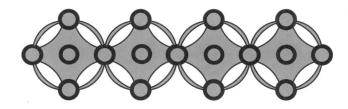

Peanut soup

Chupe de maní

Serves 4 to 6

2 tbsp peanut oil

1 onion, finely chopped

1 starchy potato, peeled and diced

1 red bell pepper, seeded and finely chopped

2 dried red chiles, seeded and crumbled

4 cups concentrated chicken or beef stock

4 tbsp finely ground toasted peanuts, plus extra peanuts for serving

salt and pepper

For serving

2 tbsp chopped fresh cilantro

diced tomato

This is a simple, quickly prepared soup popular in Ecuador and Bolivia, where the peanut, a food crop cultivated by the Incas, remains a major source of protein.

Heat the oil in a heavy-bottom saucepan over medium heat, add the onion, potato, and red bell pepper, and cook, stirring frequently, for 5 minutes, or until softened but not browned.

Stir in the chiles, add the stock, and bring to a boil. Reduce the heat and simmer gently for 15 minutes, or until well blended. Transfer half the soup to a blender or food processor, add the ground toasted peanuts, and blend to a purée. Stir back into the saucepan.

Taste and adjust the seasoning, then reheat gently. Ladle into bowls, top with a sprinkling of chopped cilantro, diced tomato, and extra peanuts, and serve.

Jerusalem artichoke soup with corn

Chupe de topinambures con elote

In this elegant soup, tender corn kernels underline the sweet earthiness of the knobbly Jerusalem artichoke tubers. The Jerusalem or root artichoke is a member of the sunflower family and native to the Americas; it is no relation of the leaf artichoke.

Serves 4 to 6

1 lb 2 oz/500 g young Jerusalem artichokes

heaping ½ cup fresh corn kernels

4 cups chicken or vegetable stock

salt

For serving

2 tbsp crumbled feta-type crumbly salty white cheese, for sprinkling

2 to 3 fresh basil sprigs, leaves stripped from the stalks and torn

1 green chile, seeded and finely chopped

fresh bread

Scrub the artichokes—there is no need to peel them—and put in a large saucepan with enough water to cover. Add salt to taste. Bring to a boil, then reduce the heat and cook until tender—test with a fork after 20 minutes. Drain, and let cool. When cool enough to handle, rub off the skins, or leave with the skins on, as you prefer.

Put the corn kernels in a saucepan with enough unsalted water to cover. Bring to a boil, then reduce the heat and cook for 2 to 3 minutes to soften the skins. Drain, reserving the cooking water.

Put the artichokes in a blender or food processor with half the corn kernels and their cooking water and the stock, then blend to a purée. Taste and adjust the seasoning, then reheat gently in a saucepan.

Ladle into bowls and top with a sprinkling of the feta-type cheese, torn basil leaves, finely chopped chile, and the remaining corn kernels. Serve with fresh bread.

Pinto bean soup with squid

Sopa seca de frijoles con calamares

Sopa seca, or "dry soup," is a broth-based dish that is drier than a soup but wetter than a stew. In this Mexican recipe, the broth is the cooking liquid from the squid. Seafood and beans is a popular combination throughout the whole region.

Serves 4 to 6

9 oz/250 g small squid

2 to 3 tbsp olive oil

1 small onion, coarsely chopped

4 to 5 garlic cloves, chopped

1 green chile, seeded and diced

2 tbsp chopped fresh epazote, or 2 tbsp chopped fresh dill and 1 tsp fennel seeds

heaping ⅓ cup dry sherry or white wine

1 lb 2 oz/500 g cooked drained pinto or cranberry beans

For serving (optional)

soft cornmeal tortillas

Rinse the squid and neatly slice if large (include the tentacles, running your fingers down the inner surface of each one to remove the little round "toenails").

Heat the oil in a saucepan, add the onion, garlic, chile, and epazote, and cook over medium heat, stirring, for 1 to 2 minutes. Add the sherry and let bubble for 2 to 3 minutes, or until the alcohol evaporates. Add the squid and cook, stirring, for 2 to 3 minutes, or until it turns opaque—don't overcook, or it will become rubbery. Remove the squid with a slotted spoon and set aside.

Add the beans to the juices in the saucepan and simmer for 5 minutes to marry the flavors. Return the squid to the saucepan and remove from the heat. Taste and add salt (no pepper is needed, as the chile is quite fiery enough).

Ladle into bowls and serve. If you like, serve with soft tortillas, cut into bite-size triangles or squares and pan-fried in a little vegetable oil until crisp, or wrapped in foil and warmed in a low oven.

Main Courses

The main meal is taken after the end of the working day in the early afternoon, allowing time to digest substantial dishes based on beans and grains, the subsistence foods of the region. In the city as well as rural areas, work begins soon after dawn and continues until it is time to return home for *merienda* at around one or two o'clock.

The rest of the day is a time for rest and enjoyment, with a light evening meal taken late. Robust bean dishes or heavy roasts are only served for lunch, while dishes that fall in between may be served both in the evening and also for lunch. Fish and vegetable dishes make an appearance as a main course in the evening or as a first course for lunch.

Chicken with almonds

Pollo en pepián

Serves 4 to 6

1 chicken, weighing 4 lb 8 oz/2 kg, cut into 12 neat pieces

lard, for cooking

1 thick slice day-old bread, cut into cubes

2 garlic cloves, chopped

2 tbsp chopped fresh cilantro

2 tbsp toasted blanched almonds

1 tsp freshly crushed allspice berries

1 tsp ground cinnamon

6 saffron strands, soaked in 1 tbsp boiling water, or 1 tsp ground turmeric

finely grated rind and juice of 1 lemon

$^2/_3$ cup dry white wine

1 onion, finely chopped

In this fragrant dish, chicken pieces are cooked in a sauce thickened with crushed almonds and flavored with allspice and saffron.

Wipe the chicken pieces and trim off any flaps of skin.

Heat the lard in a skillet, add the bread and the garlic, and cook over medium heat, turning once, for 4 to 5 minutes, or until golden.

Toss in the cilantro and cook, stirring, for a few seconds. Remove with a slotted spoon and transfer to a blender or food processor, or a mortar, with the almonds, allspice, cinnamon, saffron and its soaking water, lemon rind and juice, and wine. Blend or pound with a pestle to a thick sauce.

Add the chicken pieces and onion to the remaining lard in the skillet and cook over medium heat, turning frequently, until the chicken is lightly browned and the onion is softened—you may need to add extra lard.

Stir in the sauce and heat until bubbling. Reduce the heat, cover, and simmer gently for 20 to 30 minutes, or until the chicken is cooked through and tender. Add a little more water if the sauce dries out.

Serve warm rather than piping hot.

Black beans with shredded greens

Feijao preto

Serves 6 to 8

2 lb 4 oz/1 kg black beans

1 red onion, coarsely chopped

2 tbsp olive oil

1 green cabbage, about
2 lb 4 oz/1 kg

2 tbsp water

salt and pepper or chile flakes

For serving

4¹/₂ oz/125 g farofa (toasted manioc flour or Indian gari) or Brazil nuts, coarsely crushed and toasted in a dry skillet

Piri-piri, Tabasco sauce, or other hot sauce

about 9 oz/250 g crumbled feta cheese, (optional)

hard-cooked eggs, quartered (allow 1 per person; optional)

Suitable for vegetarians, this is a balanced dish of beans and fresh greens, eaten with assorted fiery little salsas. It is the everyday version of the Saturday *feijoada*, Brazil's national dish—a stupendous feast that takes three days to prepare.

Check over the beans and remove any tiny stones. You can presoak the beans in cold water overnight to speed up the cooking process, but this is not essential.

Drain the beans, if necessary, and put in an earthenware pot or enamel casserole with the onion and oil. Pour in enough hot water to cover the beans generously—allow at least 3 fingers' width of water above the surface of the beans. Do not add salt. Bring to a boil, then reduce the heat to low. Cover tightly and simmer for 2 hours (3 hours if the beans were very dry), or until completely tender and the skins are soft, checking regularly and adding more boiling water if necessary. Alternatively, transfer the pot to a preheated oven at 325°F/160°C, or use a pressure cooker—very popular with bean cooks—and cook for 40 minutes.

Meanwhile, trim the cabbage sparingly—remove any discolored outer leaves but leave as much of the dark green as possible. Halve the cabbage and cut out the core. Use a very

sharp knife or a food processor to shred the leaves as finely as you can. Pack the shredded leaves into a large saucepan, add the water, and bring to a boil. Cover tightly, give the saucepan a shake, and cook for 2 to 3 minutes, or until the cabbage softens slightly but retains its texture. Drain well.

Increase the heat under the beans or transfer the pot to the stove over high heat and cook to evaporate the excess water—they should not be the consistency of soup. Season with salt and pepper or chile flakes to taste.

Serve the beans in deep bowls, with the shredded cabbage and farofa and Piri-piri. Serve the crumbled cheese and hard-cooked egg quarters separately, if you like, for people to add if they please.

Sweet-sour braised pork

Pibil de carne de cerdo

This dish takes its name from the *pib*, a pit barbecue or earth oven still in use in the Yucatan. Gentle cooking in a closed pot ensures that the meat is tender. Wrapping the meat in a banana leaf gives it added flavor and gloriously sticky juices.

Serves 4 to 6

1 pork joint, weighing 4 lb 8 oz/ 2 kg, on the bone (shoulder is good)

1 1/4 cups white wine vinegar

6 garlic cloves, coarsely crushed

1 tsp peppercorns, coarsely crushed

1 tsp allspice berries, coarsely crushed

1 tsp salt

2 red bell peppers or 2 3/4 oz/75 g dried ancho chile (mild and fruity)

2 to 3 fresh red chiles or 2 3/4 oz/ 75 g dried guajillo chiles (sharp and hot)

2 to 3 tbsp boiling water (optional)

1 banana leaf, central vein removed (optional)

2 to 3 fresh or dried thyme sprigs

2 tbsp green olives

plain white rice, for serving

Relish

3 to 4 mild red onions, finely sliced

juice and finely grated rind of 1 lime

1 tsp salt

2 tbsp chopped fresh cilantro leaves

Wipe the pork joint. Slash the skin in several places with a sharp knife without cutting through to the meat and put in a large nonreactive bowl.

Put the vinegar, garlic, peppercorns, allspice, and salt in a blender or food processor and blend thoroughly. Pour the mixture over the meat, cover, and let marinate in the refrigerator for 2 hours.

Meanwhile, if using fresh red bell peppers and chiles, seed and dice. If using dried chiles, remove and discard the seeds, and soak the flesh in the boiling water for about 20 minutes to soften the flesh.

Preheat the oven to 300°F/150°C. Drain the joint, reserving the marinade. Put the marinade in the blender or food processor with the fresh bell peppers and chiles or dried chiles and their soaking water and blend to a smooth paste. Spread the paste over the meat and wrap in the banana leaf, if you have one, securing the parcel with uncolored string. Put the meat in a heavy-bottom casserole or earthenware pot into which it just fits. Tuck in the thyme sprigs and olives and add enough water to come halfway up the meat. Cover tightly.

Cook in the preheated oven for 2 to 3 hours, or until the meat is tender but not yet falling apart. Uncover, increase the oven temperature to 375°F/190°C and cook for an additional 20 minutes, or until the skin is browned and the juices have reduced to a sticky sauce.

Meanwhile, prepare the relish. Toss the onions with the lime juice and salt in a nonreactive bowl. Cover and let marinate at room temperature. Add the lime rind and cilantro.

Remove the banana leaf, then cut the meat into thick slices and serve with the onion relish and a steaming heap of plain white rice.

Baked beans with corn topping

Pastel de frijoles pintos con choclo

Serves 4 to 6

6 tbsp olive oil or butter

1 lb 10 oz/750 g onions, finely sliced

3 to 4 garlic cloves, finely chopped

1 tsp cumin seeds

1 tsp fresh or dried oregano leaves

1 lb 2 oz/500 g fresh tomatoes, peeled and chopped, or canned chopped tomatoes

1 lb 2 oz/500 g pumpkin, peeled, seeded, and cut into small dice

1 lb 10 oz/750 g cooked pinto or cranberry beans, drained

2 tbsp green olives, pitted and chopped

2 tbsp raisins

1 tbsp confectioners' sugar

1 tsp dried chile flakes

salt and pepper

Topping

2³/4 pints/1.5 litres fresh or frozen corn kernels

heaping 1¹/2 cups milk

1 egg, beaten

Red beans in a spicy tomato sauce are baked under a crisp topping of puréed corn in this vegetarian recipe from the Chilean highlands.

Heat 4 tablespoons of the oil in a heavy-bottom saucepan, add the onions and garlic, and cook over very low heat, stirring occasionally, for 20 to 30 minutes, or until the onions are softened and golden but not browned.

Add the cumin seeds, oregano, and tomatoes and heat until bubbling, mashing the tomatoes down with a potato masher, for 10 minutes, or until you have a thick, sticky sauce.

Add the pumpkin and heat until bubbling. Reduce the heat to low, cover, and cook for an additional 10 to 15 minutes, or until the pumpkin is softened but not collapsed. Stir in the beans, olives, and raisins. Reheat gently and simmer for 5 minutes to marry the flavors. Season with salt and pepper to taste.

Meanwhile, preheat the oven to 350°F/180°C. Put the corn kernels in a blender or food processor with the milk and blend to a purée.

Transfer to a saucepan and cook, stirring continuously, for 5 minutes, or until the mixture has thickened slightly. Remove from the heat and let cool to finger heat. Stir in the egg and season with salt and pepper to taste.

Spread the bean mixture in an earthenware gratin dish (or use individual baking dishes) and top with a thick layer of the corn mixture—the bean base and the topping should be of roughly equal thickness. Drizzle with the remaining oil or dot small pieces of butter over the surface and sprinkle with the sugar and chile flakes.

Bake in the preheated oven for 30 minutes, or until browned and bubbling. Serve hot.

Chicken with chile and chocolate

Pollo en mole

Serves 6 to 8

1 whole garlic bulb

1 chicken, weighing 4 lb 8 oz/2 kg

4 fresh mint sprigs

1/2 tsp black peppercorns

2 to 3 cloves

salt

Sauce

3 to 4 tbsp olive oil (lard is traditional)

1 large onion, finely sliced

1 ripe plantain or unripe banana

1 red bell pepper, seeded and diced

1 lb 2 oz/500 g fresh or canned tomatoes, peeled and chopped

3/4 cup blanched almonds or peanuts, toasted and crushed

1 tsp cumin seeds

1 tsp allspice berries

1 soft cornmeal tortilla, torn into pieces, or 1 tbsp tortilla chips

13/4 oz/50 g dried chiles, soaked in boiling water for 20 minutes, and drained (soaking water reserved)

2 tbsp raisins

finely grated rind of 1 orange

2 tbsp unsweetened cocoa or 13/4 oz/50 g semisweet chocolate

For serving

warm cornmeal tortillas

guacamole

In this classic Mexican party dish, gently poached chicken pieces are finished in a *mole* (pronounced *moll-ay*), a spicy chili sauce flavored with cocoa, which takes its name from the mortar in which the flavorings are crushed.

Score round the center of the garlic bulb. Cut the chicken into 12 neat pieces, rinse, and put in a large saucepan with enough cold water to cover generously—about heaping 61/3 cups. Bring to a boil, skimming off the foam, then add the garlic, mint sprigs, peppercorns, cloves, and a little salt. Return to a boil, then reduce the heat, cover, and simmer gently for 30 to 40 minutes, or until the chicken is tender. Remove the chicken pieces and set aside. When cool enough to handle, remove the skin, if you like. Strain the stock and set aside.

Meanwhile, for the sauce, heat 2 tablespoons of the oil in a large skillet, add the onion, and cook over low heat, stirring occasionally, for 10 to 15 minutes, or until softened and golden. Remove with a slotted spoon and set aside. Peel the plantain and cut into chunks. Reheat the oily juices in the skillet, add the red bell pepper, and cook for 5 to 6 minutes, or until softened but not browned. Add the tomatoes and plantain and heat until bubbling, then reduce the heat, cover, and cook over low heat for 20 minutes, or until the plantain is tender.

Heat a dry skillet over medium-high heat, add the nuts and spices, and cook, shaking frequently, for 3 to 4 minutes, or until toasted, being careful not to burn them. Transfer to a food processor and pulse briefly. Set aside.

Tip the onions and the tomato mixture into a blender or food processor. Seed the dried chiles, then add the tortilla and chiles and their soaking water and blend until smooth—you may need to add a little of the reserved chicken stock.

Add the remaining oil to the large skillet and reheat. Add the crushed nuts and spices and cook, stirring, for 1 to 2 minutes, to develop the flavors. Add the tomato mixture and heat until bubbling, then reduce the heat and cook gently for 5 minutes. Add the raisins, orange rind, and 4 cups of the reserved chicken stock. Bring to a boil, then reduce the heat and simmer gently for 20 minutes, or until the sauce thickens and the liquid is reduced by a third. Meanwhile, preheat the oven to 350°F/180°C.

Stir the cocoa into the sauce and heat gently without boiling.

Pour the sauce over the chicken in an ovenproof dish, cover with foil, and cook in the preheated oven for 20 to 25 minutes. Serve with warm tortillas and guacamole.

Bean casserole with potatoes, corn, and pumpkin

Cocido limeño

Serves 4 to 6

1³/4 cups lima beans

1 lb 2 oz/500 g yellow-fleshed potatoes, peeled and cubed

1 lb 2 oz/500 g pumpkin or butternut squash, seeded and cubed

18 fl oz/500 ml fresh or frozen corn kernels

salt and pepper

Flavoring salsa

2 to 3 yellow or red chiles, seeded and chopped

1 small onion, finely chopped

6 scalions, green parts included, finely chopped

2 to 3 garlic cloves, finely chopped

2 tbsp olive oil

For serving

2 tbsp fresh basil leaves, chopped

2 tbsp crumbled feta cheese

This dish is made with the plump, creamy new season lima beans, which appear in Peruvian markets just before Christmas. Satisfying and delicious, it does not include meat and is traditionally served at the fasting supper of Christmas Eve.

Soak the beans in cold water overnight. Drain and transfer to a large saucepan with enough water to cover by 2 fingers' width. Do not add salt. Bring to a boil, then reduce the heat and simmer very gently for 1½ to 2 hours, or until the beans are tender.

Meanwhile, put all the salsa ingredients in a small saucepan and cook over medium heat, stirring frequently, for 5 minutes to marry the flavors. Set aside.

When the beans are tender, add the potatoes and pumpkin and top off with enough boiling water to submerge all the ingredients. Return to a boil, then reduce the heat, cover, and cook gently for 20 to 30 minutes, or until the vegetables are tender. Season to taste.

Stir in the corn kernels and reheat until bubbling. Stir in the salsa and cook for an additional 10 minutes to marry the flavors and reduce the cooking juices. The dish should be juicy but not soupy. Sprinkle with the chopped basil and crumbled cheese and serve immediately.

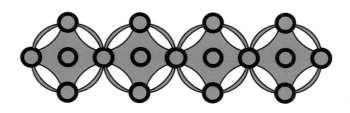

Chicken with shrimp, cashews, and coconut

Ximxim de galinha

Serves 4 to 6

1 chicken, weighing 4 lb 8 oz/2 kg, cut into 12 neat pieces

1 lb/450 g fresh tomatoes, peeled and diced, or canned chopped tomatoes

1 onion, finely sliced

2 to 3 fresh mint sprigs

1 lb/450 g raw peeled shrimp or large shrimp

1 1/4 cups canned coconut milk

sea salt

Vatapa salsa

3 1/2 oz/100 g dried shrimp or 6 oz/175 g small cooked peeled shrimp

scant 3/4 cup toasted cashews and/or peanuts

1 onion, coarsely chopped

1 heaping tbsp grated fresh ginger

4 tbsp dende oil or olive oil and a pinch ground saffron or turmeric

For serving

lime quarters

Piri-piri or Tabasco sauce

plain white rice

From Brazil, this one-stop dish features *vatapa*, a bread-thickened dipping sauce usually made with the semidried shrimp of Bahia and eaten in much the same way as a mayonnaise, used to thicken the cooking juices.

Wipe over the chicken pieces and put in a large saucepan with the tomatoes, onion, mint sprigs, and enough water to cover. Bring to a boil, then reduce the heat, cover loosely, and simmer for 20 to 30 minutes, or until the chicken is cooked through but not yet tender. Remove the mint sprigs. Remove the chicken joints, and when cool enough to handle, remove the skin. Set aside.

Reheat the tomato mixture until bubbling and cook for 6 to 8 minutes, or until reduced to a jammy sauce. Add the shrimp, let bubble up again, and cook for 1 to 2 minutes, or until curled and pink. Remove from the heat.

Meanwhile, make the salsa. Put the dried shrimp and nuts in a food processor and process briefly. Add the onion and ginger and process again until reduced to a thick paste.

Heat the oil and saffron in a large skillet, add the paste, and cook over medium heat, stirring, for 2 to 3 minutes, or until the onion is slightly softened and a fragrant steam rises. Add the chicken pieces, turning until thoroughly coated with the paste. Pour in enough water to come halfway up the chicken pieces and bring to a boil. Reduce the heat and season with a little salt. Cover loosely and simmer gently for 10 minutes, or until the chicken is tender and the flavors are well blended.

Combine the tomato and shrimp mixture with the chicken mixture, stir in the coconut milk, and reheat gently. Check the seasoning. Serve with lime quarters, Piri-piri, and plain white rice.

Baked sea bass with sweet potato, corn, and butternut squash

Corvina a la chorillana

Serves 4 to 6

1 large sea bass, weighing about
4 lb 8 oz/2 kg, cleaned and scaled

1 lb 2 oz /500 g sweet potatoes,
peeled and cut into chunks

1 lb 2 oz/500 g butternut squash,
peeled and cut into chunks

1 lb 2 oz/500 g corn on the cob,
chopped into thick slices

1 lb 2 oz/500 g shallots or small
onions, quartered lengthwise

1 glass dry white wine

3 to 4 tbsp olive oil

2 to 3 fresh or dried chiles, seeded
and chopped

sea salt

This is the Peruvian way to cook the best fish of the catch. Any firm-fleshed fish suitable for baking will do, such as salmon, monkfish, or tuna.

Preheat the oven to 350°F/180°C.

Wipe the fish and sprinkle it lightly with salt all over, including the cavity. Set aside at room temperature.

Arrange the vegetables in a roasting pan and pour in the wine. Drizzle with the oil and sprinkle with the chiles and salt to taste. Cover with foil, shiny-side down. Bake in the preheated oven for 20 minutes, or until the vegetables are nearly tender—test with a knife.

Remove the foil and place the fish on the bed of vegetables. Drizzle with a spoonful of the cooking juices, replace the foil, and bake for an additional 10 minutes, or until the fish is cooked right through. It is ready when it feels firm to the touch. Remove and let stand for an additional 10 minutes before serving, for the heat to penetrate right through to the bone.

Pot-roast beef with Guatemalan rice

Carne en jocon con arroz guatemalteco

Guatemala's succulent beef casserole is made with *tomatillos*, which resemble green tomatoes, although they are actually part of the physalis family. If you can't find tomatillos, use ordinary tomatoes and include the grated rind and juice of a lemon.

Serves 4 to 6

3 lb 5 oz/1.5 kg boned stewing beef, tied in a single piece

4 tbsp olive oil

4 garlic cloves, peeled but kept whole

2 large onions, finely chopped

1 lb 2 oz/500 g carrots, scraped and cut into chunks

2 fresh green or dried red chiles, seeded and chopped

1 tsp crumbled dried oregano

1 lb 2 oz/500 g fresh red tomatoes, peeled, seeded, and coarsely chopped, or canned chopped tomatoes

1 lb 2 oz/500 g fresh tomatillos, husks removed and chopped, or canned tomatillos

1 tbsp chopped fresh cilantro leaves, for garnishing

salt and pepper

Guatemalan rice

4 tbsp olive oil

1 lb 2 oz/500 g white long-grain rice

2 garlic cloves, chopped

1 tbsp diced celery

1 tbsp diced green bell pepper

2 tbsp diced tomato

handful of fresh or frozen peas

Wipe the stewing beef and season with salt and pepper to taste.

Heat the oil in a flameproof casserole into which the joint fits comfortably, add the garlic cloves, onions and carrots and cook over medium heat, stirring frequently, until lightly colored. Remove with a slotted spoon, draining the oil back into the casserole, and set aside. Add the meat and cook, turning frequently, until browned on all sides. Add the chiles and oregano and cook, stirring, for an additional minute.

Add the tomatoes and tomatillos and enough water to come three-quarters of the way up the meat. Season with salt and pepper to taste and bring to a boil. Reduce the heat, cover tightly, using a piece of foil as well as the lid, and simmer very gently for 1 1/2 to 2 hours, or until the meat is perfectly tender. Alternatively, transfer the casserole to a preheated oven at 300°F/150°C. You shouldn't need to add extra liquid, but if you do, add the bare minimum and make sure that it is boiling.

Meanwhile, make the rice. Heat the oil in a large skillet, add the rice, garlic, celery, and green bell pepper and cook over medium heat, stirring, for 3 to 4 minutes, or until the rice grains turn transparent. Add the tomato and enough water to cover by a finger-width's depth. Bring to a boil and season with salt and pepper to taste, then reduce the heat and cook gently for 15 to 20 minutes, or until the grains are just tender. Stir in the peas and cook for an additional 2 to 3 minutes.

When the meat is perfectly tender and the juices reduced to a sticky sauce, transfer the meat to a warmed serving dish and let rest for 10 minutes. Cut into thick slices and serve with the cooking juices, scattered with the cilantro. Serve with the rice.

Braised lamb with garlic and orange

Seco de carnero

Serves 4 to 6

1 boned, rolled shoulder of lamb,
weighing 3 lb 5 oz to 4 lb 8 oz/
1.5 to 2 kg

12 to 18 garlic cloves, unpeeled

finely grated rind and juice of
2 bitter oranges or 1 lemon and
1 sweet orange

1/2 tsp allspice berries, crushed

short length of cinnamon stick,
coarsely crushed

2/3 cup dry white wine

large handful of fresh cilantro leaves

2 green chiles, seeded and coarsely
chopped

salt and pepper

For serving

corn on the cob, chopped into
thick slices

butternut squash, peeled and cut
into chunks

This is a Peruvian method of cooking a shoulder of lamb or kid, which benefits from slow, lengthy cooking to soften the meat and tame the garlic, melting it into a delicious, gentle sauce.

Wipe the meat and season with salt and pepper to taste. Put into a flameproof casserole into which it just fits neatly. Pack the garlic cloves around the side. Scatter over the orange rind, allspice, and cinnamon and drizzle with the orange juice. Add the wine and enough water to come halfway up the meat. Bring to a boil, then reduce the heat, cover tightly, using a piece of foil as well as the lid, and simmer very gently for 1 1/2 to 2 hours, or until the meat is perfectly tender. Alternatively, transfer the casserole to a preheated oven at 300°F/150°C. Check every now and again, adding a little boiling water if the juices are drying out.

Transfer the meat to a warmed serving dish. Squeeze the garlic flesh from the skins into a blender or food processor, add the cilantro, chiles, and cooking juices, and blend to a purée. Return to the casserole and reheat gently, diluting with boiling water if necessary.

Carve the lamb into thick slices and serve with corn on the cob, butternut squash and the sauce.

Vegetable Dishes and Salads

In pre-Columbian traditions as well as the Hispanic kitchen, vegetables are treated as dishes in their own right rather than as side dishes. Since vegetables are served as a separate course or the centerpiece of a light meal, attention is paid to nutritional balance.

Where there is no meat or fish, protein is often included in the form of nuts or dairy products together with a starch food by way of accompaniment. Depending on the region, this might be cornmeal tortillas, *arepas* (thick tortillas made with white cornmeal), *patacones* (plantain chips), or chunks of fresh corn cobs. And in rural areas and regions where wheat is a luxury, root vegetables take the place of bread.

Guacamole with plantain chips

Guacamole con patacones

Serves 4 to 6

2 to 3 ripe avocados (depending on size)

2 green chiles, preferably serrano, seeded and chopped

1 small onion, coarsely chopped

1 tbsp chopped fresh cilantro

1 tsp sea salt

1 large tomato, peeled, seeded, and diced

lime juice, for dressing (optional)

Plantain chips

2 firm plantains or unripe bananas

vegetable oil, for cooking

salt

In Mexico and Central America, the avocado's place of origin, a guacamole is never a smooth purée—it is lumpy, with all elements visible. Here it is teamed with plantain chips, *patacones* or *tostones*, a popular snack in the banana-growing regions.

For the plantain chips, slice the plantains as thick as your thumb, then drop into salted water and let soak for 30 minutes, or until you can push the flesh out of the skins. Drain and pat dry.

Meanwhile, halve the avocados lengthwise, remove the pits, reserving one, and scoop the flesh into a bowl. Coarsely chop with a knife.

Put the chiles, onion, cilantro, and salt in a blender or food processor and blend to a purée.

Fold the purée into the avocados in the bowl, then stir in the tomato. Insert the reserved avocado pit in the center of the mixture to slow down the inevitable browning—it sounds odd but it seems to work! If you prepare the guacamole well ahead of serving, dress it with lime juice as an added precaution against browning—this changes the delicate balance of flavor, but some people like the touch of sharpness.

Over medium-high heat, heat enough oil to submerge the plantain slices in a large skillet—they need plenty of room. Wait until a faint blue haze rises from the oil. Add the slices, in small batches, and cook over medium heat for 4 to 5 minutes, or until fairly soft but not yet crisp. Remove and drain on paper towels in a single layer. Sandwich the slices between 2 sheets of plastic wrap. Using a small cutting board or rolling pin, flatten the slices until reduced to half their thickness (you can buy a special little wooden press that performs this task quickly and easily).

Reheat the oil to 350 to 375°F/180 to 190°C, or until a cube of bread browns in 30 seconds. Add the flattened slices, in batches, to the oil and cook for 2 to 3 minutes, or until brown and crisp on the outside and still meltingly soft on the inside. Remove and drain on paper towels.

Serve the guacamole as a dip with the hot plantain chips.

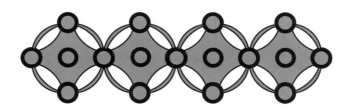

Baked large zucchini stuffed with cheese and raisins

Chancletas gratinados

In Puerto Rico they make this dish with chayote, a vine fruit that looks like a crumple-ended pale-skinned avocado—when cut, the two halves look like *chancletas*, or "little slippers," hence the name of the dish.

Serves 4 to 6

small pat of butter

8 to 12 round large zucchini or patty pan squash

²/₃ cup light cream

9 oz/250 g crumbled feta cheese

2 tbsp raisins, soaked in a little boiling water to plump up

1 tsp vanilla extract or ¹/₂ tsp seeds scraped from a vanilla bean

1 tbsp unrefined cane sugar

2 to 3 tbsp fresh white breadcrumbs

2 to 3 tbsp grated Cheddar or Gruyère cheese

Preheat the oven to 375°F/190°C. Grease a baking dish with the butter.

Rinse the large zucchini and put in a large saucepan with enough lightly salted boiling water to cover. Return to a boil, then reduce the heat and simmer for 10 minutes. Drain and let cool slightly, then slice each in half through the center. Scrape out and discard the fiber and seeds. Scrape out and set aside about a finger's width of the flesh, leaving the remainder on the skin as a liner.

Arrange the hollowed-out shells in the prepared baking dish. Put the reserved large zucchini flesh into a blender or food processor and blend to a purée with the cream. Stir in the feta-type cheese, raisins, vanilla, and sugar. Divide the mixture among the shells. Mix the breadcrumbs with the grated Cheddar cheese and sprinkle over the stuffing.

Bake in the preheated oven for 20 to 25 minutes, or until the cheese has melted and the topping is crisp and brown. Serve immediately.

Gratin of green chiles with cream and cheese

Rajas poblanas

Serves 4 to 6

1 lb 10 oz/750 g thin-fleshed, mild green chiles, preferably Anaheim

heaping 1 cup light cream

heaping 1 cup heavy cream

9 oz/250 g crumbled feta cheese

salt and pepper

soft cornmeal tortillas, for serving

This is an everyday dish that everyone knows how to cook and no one bothers with a recipe for. The utterly delicious combination of peppery, lemony chiles, and sweet, rich cream offers the perfect balance of texture and flavor.

Wipe the chiles, but don't remove the stalks or seeds. Using tongs, hold the chiles over a gas flame, or cook under a preheated broiler or oven on the highest setting, until the skins are black and blistered in places. Transfer to a plastic or paper bag and let stand for 10 minutes to loosen the skins. Remove the skins. Slice the flesh into ribbons (rajas) and arrange in a gratin dish.

Meanwhile, heat the cream in a small saucepan and remove it as soon as it reaches boiling point. Pour over the chile ribbons and sprinkle with the cheese. Season with a little salt and pepper—not too much, as the cheese is already salty and one or two of the chiles may be fiery.

Preheat the broiler to very high. Cook the chiles for 8 to 10 minutes, or until brown and bubbling. Meanwhile, wrap the tortillas in foil and warm through in a preheated low oven for 5 minutes. Serve the gratin piping hot with the warmed tortillas for mopping up.

Baked sweet potato with garlic salsa

Batata con mojo

Serves 4 to 6

2 lb 4 oz/1 kg sweet potatoes

2 tbsp chopped fresh cilantro, for sprinkling

Mojo dressing

2 tbsp olive oil

4 garlic cloves, crushed

juice of 3 to 4 oranges (about 2/3 cup)

juice and grated rind of 1 lemon

1/2 tsp sea salt

This simple country dish is popular in Cuba. Ring the changes with plantain, cassava, pumpkin, potatoes, or any plain-cooked vegetables.

Preheat the oven to 350°F/180°C.

Wash the sweet potatoes and pat dry. Bake in the preheated oven for 40 minutes, then test for softness with a knife—they may take up to an additional 20 minutes to cook, depending on their variety and shape.

Meanwhile, make the dressing. Heat the oil and garlic in a small saucepan, add the citrus juices, lemon rind, and salt, and let bubble for 3 to 4 minutes, or until blended.

When the sweet potatoes are perfectly tender, remove from the oven. When cool enough to handle, remove the skins and dice the flesh into bite-size pieces.

Fold the diced sweet potato into the dressing. Serve at room temperature with the chopped cilantro sprinkled over.

New potatoes with tomato, cheese, and eggs

Pipián

Serves 4 to 6

2 lb 4 oz/1 kg small new yellow-fleshed potatoes, scrubbed

2 to 3 hard-cooked eggs, peeled

2 tbsp butter

1 onion, finely chopped

1 lb 2 oz/500 g tomatoes, peeled, seeded, and diced, or 3 tbsp canned crushed tomatoes

2/3 cup heavy cream

5 1/2 oz/150 g mild cheddar-type cheese, grated

salt

For serving

2 tbsp roasted unsalted peanuts, coarsely crushed

1 tsp dried chile flakes

Here, a creamy cheese and tomato sauce is poured over potatoes and eggs, with a sprinkling of crushed peanuts. In Peru, where this dish originates, it is made with *papas criollas*, nutty little yellow-fleshed potatoes that can be eaten in a single bite.

Cook the potatoes in their skins in a large saucepan of salted water for 15 to 20 minutes, or until tender. Drain the potatoes thoroughly and transfer to a warmed serving dish. Cut the hard-cooked eggs into quarters and arrange them among the potatoes.

Meanwhile, heat the butter in a large skillet. As soon as it is foaming, add the onion and cook over low heat, stirring frequently, for 10 minutes, or until softened and golden. Add the tomatoes and heat until bubbling, mashing to blend. Cook, stirring, for an additional 5 minutes. Stir in the cream, let bubble up again, and add the cheese. Continue to cook, stirring, until the cheese melts and the sauce is pink and smooth. Taste and add salt if necessary.

Pour the sauce over the potatoes and eggs, sprinkle with the peanuts and chile flakes, and serve immediately.

Shrimp salad with chicken and palm hearts

Salata de palmito, frango e camarón

This simple salad is popular in Brazil, where the edible palm is widely cultivated as a crop. If palm hearts are unavailable either canned or fresh, substitute kohlrabi, cut into thin sticks, or shredded white cabbage—texture matters as much as flavor.

Serves 4 to 6

1 lb/450 g fresh or canned palm or artichoke hearts

5$^1/_2$ oz/150 g cooked peeled shrimp

5$^1/_2$ oz/150 g cooked chicken breast, shredded

1 small romaine lettuce, shredded

1 tbsp fresh or toasted finely shredded coconut

Dressing

6 tbsp olive oil

2 tbsp lime or lemon juice

few drops of Piri-piri or Tabasco sauce

1 tsp sea salt

Beat the dressing ingredients together in a nonreactive bowl.

If the palm hearts are fresh, trim off any remnants of the fibrous exterior and use the slicing device on a box grater to give you long, thin ribbons like tagliatelle. If canned, drain and slice thinly in the same way.

Combine the palm hearts with the dressing in the bowl, cover, and let marinate at room temperature for 1 to 2 hours.

Add the shrimp and chicken to the bowl and toss to combine. Heap on to a bed of shredded lettuce, then sprinkle with the coconut.

Quinoa and corn paella with mint

Picada de quinua

Serves 4 to 6

1 lb/450 g quinoa

2 tbsp olive oil

2 to 3 garlic cloves, chopped

2 red or yellow chiles (preferably native to the Andes), seeded and finely chopped

1 large tomato, peeled, seeded, and diced

2 tbsp fresh or frozen corn kernels

1 tbsp fresh mint leaves

salt (optional)

romaine lettuce leaves, for serving

Quinoa (pronounced *keenwa*) is a highly nutritious grain native to the Amazonian highlands. This nutty little seed has a semitransparent shell that pops when cooked. The leaves are also edible and make an excellent substitute for spinach.

Put the quinoa in a strainer and rinse under cold running water until the water runs clear.

Transfer the quinoa to a large saucepan and cover with double its own volume of water. Bring to a boil, then reduce the heat and simmer for 20 minutes, or until the grains have popped their shells—they will look translucent with little white curls—and have absorbed all the water.

Meanwhile, heat the oil in a large skillet, add the garlic and chile, and cook over medium heat, stirring, for 2 to 3 minutes, or until the garlic is softened. Stir in the tomato and corn, heat until bubbling, and let bubble for 1 minute.

Stir in the cooked quinoa and reheat gently to marry the flavors. Taste and add salt if necessary. Chop the mint leaves and stir into the mixture.

Serve with crisp romaine lettuce leaves for scooping. Paella is traditionally eaten from the circular pan in which it is cooked, each person eating the portion directly in front of them.

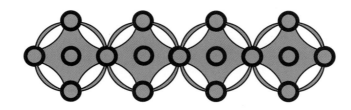

Sweet-and-sour pumpkin

Hogao de auyama

Serves 4 to 6

2 lb 4 oz/1 kg pumpkin

4 tbsp olive oil

1 large onion, finely sliced

1 to 2 hot red chiles, seeded and finely chopped

2 lb 4 oz/1 kg fresh ripe tomatoes, peeled and diced, or canned chopped tomatoes

1 tbsp golden raisins

2 tbsp red wine vinegar

finely grated rind and juice of 1 bitter orange or lemon

salt

Plantain Chips, for serving

Hogao, a slow-cooked onion and tomato sauce, is the basic flavoring of Colombia's criollo kitchen. Chunks of sweet pumpkin are added to the thick, jammy sauce in this recipe, which is sharpened with vinegar and sweetened with golden raisins.

Peel, seed, and dice the pumpkin—you will need a very sharp knife.

Heat the oil in a large saucepan, add the onion, and cook over very low heat, stirring occasionally, for at least 15 minutes, or until soft and golden but not browned. Add the chiles and tomatoes and heat until bubbling. Reduce the heat and simmer for 20 to 30 minutes, or until the ingredients reduce to a jammy sauce.

Stir in the pumpkin, golden raisins, vinegar, and orange rind and juice. Let bubble up again, then reduce the heat and cook, loosely covered, for 20 minutes, or until the flavors are well blended and the pumpkin is perfectly tender. Serve at room temperature with crisp Plantain Chips.

Corn on the cob with two salsas

Maiz tierno asado con dos salsas

Serves 4 to 6

8 to 12 corn on the cob in their husks

Chimichurri

1 small mild red onion, diced

4 garlic cloves, finely chopped

4 tbsp finely chopped fresh flat-leaf parsley

1 tsp fresh thyme leaves

finely grated rind and juice of 2 lemons

heaping 1 cup olive oil

Piri-piri

3½ oz/100 g hot red chiles, preferably malagueta

3½ oz/100 g red bell peppers

heaping ⅓ cup white wine vinegar

1 tsp sea salt

Corn cobs left in their husks—nature's wrapper—taste all the better when allowed to cook in their own steam. They are ideal served with a couple of dipping salsas—a mild *chimichurri* and a fiery *piri-piri*.

First make the salsas. Pack all the ingredients for the chimichurri into a screw-top jar. Screw on the lid, shake, and then let infuse at room temperature for 1 to 2 hours, or overnight in the refrigerator.

To make the piri-piri, remove the stalks from the chiles (rinse your fingers after handling them and don't rub your eyes). Seed and coarsely chop the red bell peppers. Heat the vinegar with an equal quantity of water and the salt in a small saucepan over medium heat, stirring until the salt has dissolved. Pour the hot vinegar into a blender or food processor, add the chiles and red pepper, and blend to a purée. Let cool—it is ready to serve as soon as it has cooled.

Pull off the silky tassel at the top of each corn cob, keeping the leaves intact. Light a barbecue, preheat a broiler to medium-high, or preheat the oven to 400°F/200°C.

Cook the corn cobs on the barbecue, under the preheated broiler, or in the preheated oven, turning frequently, for 8 to 12 minutes. If cooking on the barbecue or under the broiler, sprinkle the husks with water from your fingers if they start to blacken.

Serve the corn cobs in their husks, with the salsas separately. Encourage your guests to chop the cobs into thick slices for dipping into the salsas.

Plantain and eggplant ratatouille

Boronia de platano

Serves 4 to 6

1 lb 2 oz/500 g ripe plantains or unripe bananas, sliced

1 lb 2 oz/500 g firm eggplants, diced

4 to 5 tbsp olive oil

2 shallots or red onions, finely sliced

2 large carrots, scraped and diced

1 to 2 celery stalks, chopped

2 garlic cloves, coarsely chopped

2 to 3 dried chiles, seeded and torn

1 tsp cumin seeds

salt and pepper

For serving

1 tbsp fresh basil leaves, coarsely torn

5½ oz /150 g crumbled feta cheese (optional)

Prepared in a similar way to a Provençal ratatouille, this dish consists of a combination of vegetables that complement each other, flavored with chile and cumin. The vegetables should be more or less matched in size and shape.

Soak the plantains in a bowl of salted water for 10 minutes to loosen the skins. Push the plantain flesh out of the skins. Cook in a saucepan of lightly salted boiling water for 20 to 25 minutes, or until tender but not mushy. Drain and set aside.

Meanwhile, put the eggplant in a colander, sprinkle with salt, and let the juices drain.

Heat the oil in a heavy-bottom flameproof casserole, add the shallots, and cook over very low heat, stirring occasionally, for at least 20 minutes, or until softened and golden but not browned. Remove with a slotted spoon, draining the oil back into the casserole, and set aside. Add the carrots and celery and cook over medium heat, stirring occasionally, for about 10 minutes, or until softened. Remove with a slotted spoon and set aside.

Rinse the eggplant under cold running water and pat dry. Reheat the casserole, add the garlic, eggplant, chiles, and cumin seeds and cook over medium heat, stirring frequently, for about 15 minutes, or until the eggplant softens and caramelizes slightly—you may need to add a little more oil. Stir in the plantain slices, shallots, and carrot and celery, and turn everything in the oily juices.

Cook over low heat, stirring, for an additional 5 minutes to marry the flavors. Season with salt and pepper to taste.

Serve warm or cool—never chilled—scattered with the torn basil leaves and the crumbled cheese, if using.

Desserts

Sweet dishes are relatively new to the region, since sugar was not known in the Americas until sugar cane plantations were established in the Caribbean in the colonial period. The taste-enhancer for fruit was (and still is) a dusting of fiery chile, a seasoning used for at least 5,000 years. The only source of sweetness was wild-gathered honeycomb.

Plant foods native to the region include chocolate, an infusion made with the fermented sun-dried seeds of a small forest tree, and vanilla, the seed pods of a white-flowered tree orchid. These homegrown flavorings quickly made their way into the pastries and custards that arrived in the New World as the specialty of Spanish and Portuguese nuns.

Caramel pineapple custards

Flan de piña

Makes 4 to 6

Caramel

3 tbsp superfine sugar

3 tsp water

juice of ½ lemon

Custard

1¼ cups pineapple juice

1¼ cups granulated sugar

6 large egg yolks (add an extra 2 if the eggs are small)

For serving (optional)

4 to 6 tbsp diced ripe papaya or mango

1 tbsp fresh mint leaves

In this popular milk and egg dessert—Latin American children love it as much as they do in Spain—the milk is replaced with the juice of a fresh pineapple, which is native to the Amazonian lowlands.

Preheat the oven to 350°F/180°C.

Make the caramel. Using a wooden spoon, stir the superfine sugar into the water and lemon juice in a heavy-bottom saucepan, bring to a boil over high heat, and cook for a few seconds, until the water evaporates completely and the sugar turns a rich golden brown. Remove from the heat, let cool briefly, then divide the caramel between 4 to 6 individual custard molds or soufflé dishes. Roll it around to coat the bases. Set aside to cool.

To make the custard, put the pineapple juice and granulated sugar in a heavy-bottom saucepan and heat gently, stirring with a wooden spoon, until the sugar has dissolved. Increase the heat and boil steadily for 15 minutes, or until the volume has reduced by a third. It is ready when the syrup leaves a transparent trail when you lift the spoon.

Meanwhile, put the egg yolks in a blender or food processor and blend thoroughly or beat with a hand-held whisk until well blended. Add the hot syrup in a steady stream with the motor running or beat in vigorously with the whisk. Pour the mixture into the prepared mold or dishes. Transfer to a roasting pan and pour in enough water to come halfway up the sides. Cover with foil, shiny-side down.

Bake the custards in the preheated oven for 30 to 40 minutes, depending on the size of the molds, or until set—they are ready when firm to the touch.

Let cool before unmolding: run a knife around the side of the mold or dish, lay a plate over the top, and invert both plate and mold. Serve with papaya or mango and mint, if you like—the gentle flavors complement the smoothness and sharpness of the pineapple.

Passion fruit and rum granita

Granita de caipirinha de maracujá

Makes about 6 cups

12 ripe passion fruit

1³/₄ cups unrefined cane sugar

about 4 cups water

cachaça or white rum

maraschino cherries, for serving (optional)

Brazil's famous rum cocktail, in its everyday form, is a potent mix of *cachaça*—sugar cane rum—and lime juice poured over ice. Here, as served at every fashionable cocktail party in Rio, it is made with fresh passion fruit juice.

To prepare the passion fruit juice, make a small hole in the leathery skin of each passion fruit and squeeze the seeds and surrounding jelly and juice into a strainer set over a bowl. Press the pulp firmly with a wooden spoon to extract all the liquid—you need about 1 heaping cup (do not use more—it is very strong).

Put the sugar with half the water in a heavy-bottom saucepan. Bring gently to a boil, stirring until the sugar has dissolved. Let cool, then stir in the passion fruit juice and dilute with the remaining water to taste.

Pour the mixture into a very well-scrubbed baking sheet and freeze for 30 minutes. Scrape the firm outer parts into the soft center and freeze again. Repeat every 30 minutes, or until firm enough to form a spoonable slush.

Spoon the slush into long, well-chilled glasses, add a measure of cachaça, and serve with a straw. For maximum impact, add a maraschino cherry and a cocktail parasol.

To store the granita for up to 3 months, transfer to a lidded plastic freezerproof container. Remove from the freezer 20 minutes before you are ready to serve and scrape it again as soon as it softens.

Sweet potato and pecan banana bread

Pan de batata

Serves 6 to 8

9 oz/250 g mashed cooked sweet potato, preferably boniatillo

9 oz/250 g very ripe bananas, peeled and cut into chunks

2 eggs, beaten

1³/4 cups self-rising flour

1 tsp baking powder

1 tsp ground allspice

9 tbsp butter, softened, plus extra for greasing

scant ³/4 cup brown sugar

1 cup pecans or walnuts, coarsely broken

This is a Cuban version of the Caribbean's favorite cut-and-come-again cake; not only every island but every household treasures its own particular recipe. The main flavoring is allspice, the berries of a small forest tree native to the Caribbean.

Preheat the oven to 350°F/180°C. Grease and line a 9 x 6-inch/23 x 15-cm loaf pan with greased wax paper—the bread is rather sticky.

Put the sweet potato, bananas, and eggs in a blender or food processor and blend to a purée. Set aside.

Sift the flour with the baking powder and allspice and set aside.

Using a wooden spoon, beat the butter with the sugar in a warmed bowl until pale and fluffy. Alternatively, process in a food processor. Switching to a metal spoon, gently fold the sweet potato and banana mixture into the butter and sugar mixture. Fold in the flour mixture until you have a smooth cake batter that drops easily from the spoon—you may need to loosen it with a little hot water. Fold in the nuts.

Pour the mixture into the prepared loaf pan, spreading it well into the corners. Bake in the preheated oven for 1 hour, or until well risen and springy in the center and the cake shrinks away from the sides. It may need a little longer to bake, in which case reduce the oven temperature to 325°F/160°C and bake for an additional 10 to 15 minutes.

Turn out on to a cooling rack to cool. Serve at room temperature in slices. The bread can be stored in an airtight container for 3 to 4 days.

Tropical fruit salad with chili syrup

Dulce de frutas tropicales

Serves 4 to 6

1 ripe papaya, peeled, seeded, and diced

1 ripe mango, seeded and diced

1 small ripe pineapple, peeled, cored, and diced

½ cup unrefined cane sugar

heaping 1 cup water

2 to 3 hot fresh or dried red chiles

2 to 3 fresh basil sprigs (optional), for decorating

Chile is traditional with fruit, heightening its natural sweetness and stimulating the taste buds. Fresh fruit cut into chunks to order is Mexico's favorite street food, and it always comes with an offer of the chili shaker as well as the sugar bowl.

Fold the prepared fruit together in a bowl and sprinkle with half the sugar.

Put the remaining sugar with the water in a small saucepan. Bring gently to a boil, stirring until the sugar has dissolved. Add the chiles, return to a boil, and bubble for 5 minutes, or until the volume is reduced by a third. Remove from the heat and let infuse for 30 minutes.

Remove the chiles and pour the syrup over the fruit, folding gently to blend. Serve decorated with the basil sprigs, if you like, and a few slivers of the syrupy chiles.

Cherimoya sherbet with coffee toffee sauce

Sorbete de chirimoya con dulce de cafe

Serves 6 to 8

2 lb 4 oz/1 kg ripe cherimoyas (custard apples)

juice of l lemon

scant ³/₄ cup superfine sugar

1¹/₄ cups water

Coffee toffee sauce

1³/₄ cups canned sweetened condensed milk

1¹/₂ cups canned unsweetened evaporated milk

1 heaping tbsp instant coffee granules

For serving (optional)

about 6 to 8 small macaroons, coarsely crushed

about 1³/₄ oz/50 g chocolate-coated coffee beans

Cherimoya, also known as custard apple, tastes somewhere between a banana and a pear. The pale flesh makes a smooth, delicate cream that freezes perfectly. Here it is served with *dulce de leche*, a toffee sauce.

Quarter, peel, and seed the custard apples—the hard black seeds are distributed throughout the flesh and must be discarded. Sprinkle with the lemon juice.

Put the sugar and water in a heavy-bottom saucepan. Bring gently to a boil, stirring until the sugar has dissolved, then continue to boil for 5 minutes. Let cool.

Put the custard apples in a blender or food processor with the sugar syrup and blend to a purée. Pour into an ice-making tray and freeze for 2 hours, or until solid. Scoop out and blend again in the blender or food processor. Return to the ice-making tray and refreeze for 1 to 2 hours, or until firm.

Meanwhile, make the sauce. Combine the two milks in a heavy-bottom saucepan and cook over medium heat, stirring steadily, for 20 to 30 minutes, or until thick and lightly caramelized. Stir in the coffee, making sure that the granules have dissolved, remove from the heat, and set aside. Reheat gently without boiling, just before serving.

When you are ready to serve, add the macaroons, if using, to 6 to 8 pretty glasses and spoon over the sherbet. Drizzle with the warm sauce and sprinkle with the chocolate-coated coffee beans, if using.

Winter fruit compote

Mazamorra

Serves 4 to 6

heaping ½ cup raisins

heaping ½ cup prunes

heaping ½ cup dried apricots
or figs

finely pared rind of 1 orange

scant 1¾ cup brown sugar

1 tsp allspice berries, coarsely
crushed

1 tsp chopped fresh ginger

1 finger-length piece cinnamon
stick, broken

4 cups water, plus 2 tbsp

1 small pineapple, peeled, cored,
and cut into chunks

1 level tbsp cornstarch

For serving

seeds of 1 pomegranate

2 tbsp toasted cashews or pecans

This winter fruit salad is made with dried fruit and fresh pineapple, spiced with ginger, cinnamon, and allspice and thickened with a little cornstarch—delicious served warm with cream. *Mazamorra* is particularly popular in Peru.

Put the dried fruit in a large saucepan with the orange rind, sugar, and the spices, tied in a scrap of clean cheesecloth or cloth to make a spice bag. Add the 4 cups water, stir, and bring to a boil. Reduce the heat and simmer for 30 minutes, or until the fruit is soft and juicy and the cooking juices are reduced by half. You may need to add more boiling water. Remove the spice bag and the orange rind, if you can find it.

Add the pineapple to the compote and reheat until just below boiling point. Simmer gently for 5 minutes to soften the pineapple and marry the flavors.

Meanwhile, blend the cornstarch with the 2 tablespoons water to a smooth paste.

Stir the cornstarch paste into the compote juices and heat gently, stirring continuously to avoid lumps, until the juices thicken. Remove from the heat and let cool slightly.

Transfer the compote to a glass serving dish, sprinkle with the pomegranate seeds and toasted nuts, and serve.

Papaya honeycomb mousse

Baba de lechosa

Serves 4 to 6

1 ripe papaya, about 1 lb/450 g

juice and finely pared strips of rind of 2 limes or small lemons

heaping 1/3 cup cold water, plus 2 tbsp

2 sheets clear gelatin or 1 tbsp (1/6 oz/7 g) powdered gelatin

1 1/4 cups canned unsweetened condensed milk or fresh cream

3 egg whites

6 tbsp superfine sugar

few fresh basil sprigs, for decorating (optional)

crisp wafers or semisweet chocolate finger cookies, for serving (optional)

The papaya, a tropical fruit native to Brazil, Mexico, and the Caribbean, has a peach-strawberry-banana flavor that benefits from the sharpness of citrus juice—lime, lemon, or bitter orange (the latter the regional favorite when in season).

Halve the papaya and remove the seeds in their gooey juice (set aside for decorating, if you like), scoop out the flesh, and put in a blender or food processor with the lime juice. Blend to a purée.

Put the heaping 1/3 cup water in a small saucepan and sprinkle with the gelatin (if using leaf gelatin, tear it into small pieces first). Let stand for 10 minutes, or until the gelatin softens and becomes spongy, or follow the package directions. Set the saucepan over low heat, stirring until all the granules are dissolved—there is no need to bring it to a boil. Fold in the papaya purée and the condensed milk.

Whisk the egg whites in a bowl until stiff—be careful you don't overwhisk or they will become grainy. Add 4 tablespoons of the sugar, one spoonful at a time, and continue to whisk until you have a soft meringue. Fold the meringue into the papaya purée. Spoon into a soufflé dish or divide among 4 to 6 individual soufflé dishes, cover, and let chill in the refrigerator for 2 to 3 hours until set.

Put the remaining sugar in a small saucepan with the 2 tablespoons water and stir over low heat until the sugar has dissolved. Add the lime rind, reserving some for decorating, and heat until bubbling, then reduce the heat and cook gently for 10 minutes, or until the water has all evaporated and the lime rind is tender.

Decorate the mousse with the reserved lime rind and basil sprigs, if using, just before serving. Serve with crisp little wafers or semisweet chocolate finger cookies, if you like. The reserved seeds can be crushed and used as a finishing sprinkle—the flavor is nutty and a little mustardy.

Guava creams with vanilla

Dulce de guayaba con vainilla

Serves 4 to 6

2 to 3 ripe guavas, about 1 lb/450 g total weight, cored, peeled, and cut into chunks

2 to 3 ripe bananas (depending on size), peeled and thickly sliced

1 lb 2 oz/500 g unrefined cane sugar

1 finger's length vanilla bean, split to expose the seeds

about 2 cups water

1¼ cups whipping cream or canned condensed milk

The guava, a native of Ecuador and Peru, is usually about the size of a large pear (although variable), with a subtle flowery fragrance and soft, slightly grainy flesh that varies in color from a deep rose to creamy white.

Put the guavas and bananas in a small heavy-bottom saucepan with the sugar, vanilla bean, and water—just enough to cover the fruit. Bring to a boil, then reduce the heat, cover loosely, and cook gently for 30 to 40 minutes, or until the fruit is a rich dark red and the juices thicken to a clear syrup.

Remove from the heat and let cool. Remove the vanilla bean and scrape the seeds into the juices. Transfer the fruit and syrup to a blender or food processor and blend to a purée.

Whip the cream until thick enough to hold soft peaks, and fold into the fruit purée. Transfer to a serving dish, cover, and chill in the refrigerator for at least 2 hours before serving. Alternatively, transfer to a lidded plastic freezerproof container, freeze for 2 to 3 hours, or until firm, and serve as a parfait.

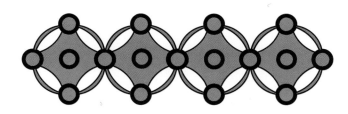

Chocolate pecan brownies with chile

Biscochitos de chocolate y nueces con chilli

Makes 12

3¹/₂ tbsp unsalted butter, softened, plus extra for greasing

¹/₂ cup unrefined cane sugar

3 eggs, beaten

³/₄ cup self-rising flour

scant 1 cup unsweetened cocoa

1 tsp dried chile flakes

about 1 tbsp rum

1 cup pecan halves

Gorgeously sticky, chewy brownies with a difference—a chile flavoring subtle enough to wake up the taste buds without shocking the palate. The Aztecs and Mayans considered their chile-flavored drinking chocolate the food of the gods.

Preheat the oven to 350°F/180°C. Grease an 8-inch/20-cm square or equivalent-size rectangular shallow baking pan or sheet.

Using a wooden spoon, beat the butter with sugar in a warmed bowl until pale and fluffy. Alternatively, process in a food processor. Beat in the eggs, a little at a time, adding a little flour if the mixture begins to curdle. Switching to a metal spoon, gently fold in the flour, cocoa, and chili flakes. Stir in the rum and add enough water until you have a cake batter that drops easily from the spoon. Taste and see if you need to add a little more chile. Fold in the pecans, setting a few of the best aside for the top.

Pour the cake batter into the prepared pan, smoothing it into the corners. Sprinkle the top with the reserved pecans.

Bake in the preheated oven for 20 to 25 minutes, or until crusted on top but still not quite set. Remove from the oven and cut into 12 squares while still warm. Transfer to a cooling rack to cool and set.

Index

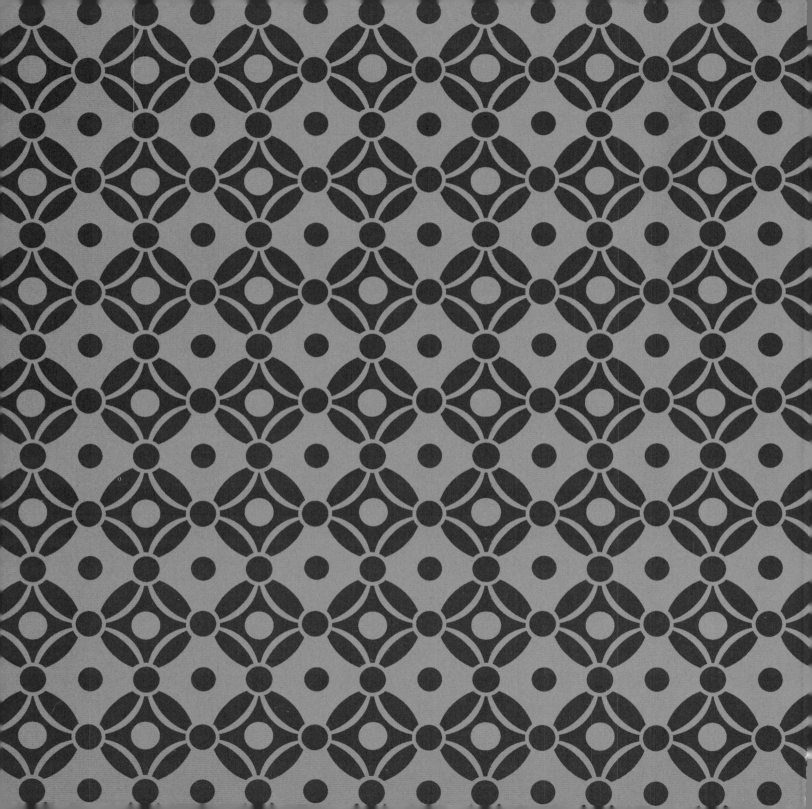